Quicksilver

poems by

Margo Davis

Finishing Line Press
Georgetown, Kentucky

Quicksilver

For Frieda, Paloma and Gus

Copyright © 2022 by Margo Davis
ISBN 978-1-64662-769-1 First Edition
All rights reserved under International and Pan-American Copyright Conventions. No part of this book may be reproduced in any manner whatsoever without written permission from the publisher, except in the case of brief quotations embodied in critical articles and reviews.

ACKNOWLEDGMENTS

Some of these poems have appeared (a few with minor changes) in hardcopy or online:

A Clean, Well-Lighted Place: "Foolish Endeavor" with a different title
Alimentum: The Literature of Food: "Why go to heaven"
Ampersand: "Dirt Poor"
Calliope: "Maternal Instinct"
Deep South Magazine: "I heard"
Houston Chronicle: "I don't appear"
Illya's Honey: "Heat Wave"
Louisiana Literature: "Imagine" and "Pacing Out the Storm"
Light Journal: "Nothing Sounds"
Main Street Rag: "Come Saturday Night"
Ocotillo Review: "Quicksilver"
Out of the Depths: "Picnic"
San Antonio Express: "I don't appear"
Snapdragon: "Suburban Tremors"
Texas Poetry Calendar: "Bacchanal"
The Ekphrastic Review: "Grey Days" and "A Child Again"
The Fourth River: "Census Bureau"
Waco Worldfest: "Fire!"
What Rough Beast: "Appropriate" and "Rupture"
Wisconsin Review: "Alternate Route"

Publisher: Leah Huete de Maines
Editor: Christen Kincaid
Cover Art: Margo Davis
Author Photo: Margo Davis
Cover Design: Elizabeth Maines McCleavy

Order online: www.finishinglinepress.com
also available on amazon.com

Author inquiries and mail orders:
Finishing Line Press
PO Box 1626
Georgetown, Kentucky 40324
USA

Table of Contents

I don't appear	1
Grey Days	2
Backyard Primer	3
Dirt Poor	4
Composure	5
Pacing out the Storm	6
Picnic	7
Maternal Instinct	8
Fire!	9
Heat Wave	10
Fifth Anniversary	11
Appropriate	12
To break the silence	13
Come Saturday	14
Suburban Tremors	15
A Child Again	16
Nothing sounds	17
Alternate Route	18
Imagine	19
Census Bureau	20
Doubt	21
Quicksilver	22
Afterglow	23
Foolish endeavor	24
Irresistible Full Moon	25
Rupture	26
Like my daughter	27
Flickering Prayer	28
Why go to heaven	29
Origin of Reason	30
I am	31
Fifty-Minute Therapy Session: Formative Years	32
I heard	33
Unexpected Guest	34
Sunset Aperitif in the Garden	35
Bacchanal	36

I don't appear

the same in this mirror
as I do in others. In the one
near the hall closet I clothe myself
in composure. In this reflection, I see
myself self-conscious,
best sly sideways pose,
smile deep as my tummy tries to tuck,
posture-perfect, sloped shoulders thrust
back. That sucked-in sideways look
meant to suck others into
liking me without its likening
my slack demeanor. Bedroom mirrors
can reflect that as I prepare
a face to meet another's
expectation. Both mine and theirs
fade after that photo-op. And in the bath,
my relaxed glance is unprepared
for this aging countenance
I encounter first and last.
Saddened by the gulf
I find between those full-length gazes
and my peppy face that greets
the glass door's reflection,
a windowpane's shadow or that
sheen from an elevator bank where I
step in and pulley a grave expression
to meet other masked
familiar faces.

Grey Days
            after Helen Levitt's 1940 photo, *Seven Young Boys*

It's black and white, this snapshot
I can't shake off. Young boys,
ranging five to eight, I would guess
not from height but seriousness,

wafer-thin, in smudged shirts
ragged as the crumbling curb
they idle near. One tyke stands

in the garbage-strewn gutter
as a neighbor boy pedals
a dented tricycle into what seems
a mirror at the center of the grimy

sidewalk. It's 1940, post-Depression
and before the ensuing war.
What sorcerer props up this

illusion? A frame minus its mirror,
no reflection, unadorned life itself,
the kid trading one reality for another.
At his back, *Walter Quay Hand Laundry*.

In his sights, a cohort out on the street.
Mere boys, too young for the draft,
caught between causes.

Backyard Primer

Mom shucks pins into a shirt tail
folded into a u-shaped pocket on her pencil-thin frame.

Her fingers braille their shapes,
her mind a blank page. Pins shower her bare feet

with each coarse groan. A few
cling tight to stiff sheets that elide into a box in low grass.

Some pins snap in two, then
separate, bereft H's and A's needing tension

to keep them together. No page
turner, this, as she stands at the clothesline, a stiff Y,

holding things together for the rest
of her alphabet, fingers clamped like pursed lips.

Let's go inside, I say a third time
before she turns a new page. Like I'm speaking

in tongues. I coax from her
the container used to link present with past. She wanders

toward the kitchen as if it holds
her place at the stove. My favorite episode: she once

conjugated a pot roast with
vegetables in a pot. As I shake out fresh sheets,

her mother's monogrammed
hankie flutters to the floor. Mother's consonants

give way to hollow vowels.
She searches an empty pot for what has passed.

I wait for the next installment.

Dirt Poor

The lake is really a slate roof. A duck
gliding across the smooth surface
is a plastic bag gulping hot air.
The duck's path, a power line gone slack.
If I squint, my shadow forms a storm cloud,
the whiff of creosote forecasts rain
and that strewn hub cap that rap-taps
across the pock-marked highway, music
to my tapping foot. Sunlight glances off
the pie tin dancing in the bare-bones
fig tree. A curious blue jay won't mistake
bed sheets whipping the clothesline
for thunderclap clap-snapping.
It's not raindrops landing on fault
lines in my garden that I watch for.
It's something less essential, more.

Composure

Mother posed behind me,
arms draped over and down
my rosebud chest. An onlooker might think
her posture reassuring,

a life vest for her young daughter.
But by eleven it was I who protected,
an oval shield wider than her slim presence,
her expression casual as a fox-trim coat

artfully slung across a chair.
At core, rocky soil
holding my dandelion roots
in place. My first wobbly tooth,

offered up for a touch of fairy dust,
a magic coin. Ignored.

So bright, that first shock,
blood staining my panties. Aching
change. What's wrong with me?
My budding body signaling a future

that might hold a baby I could
ignore, too, dress for a wholesome family
snapshot. How I yearned to break
free from such a grasp, go anywhere

at all, for any length of time,
to drift and wobble, to revolve
around anyone, to stain my reputation
or never have one.

Pacing out the Storm

Her eyes dart to the last page in an untidy mystery
when the lights whisk out the back door with a bang.
A lightning bolt proves too quick
to catch the denouement.

The moon stumbles in fog.
Her flashlight stammers and faints.
In a bottomless drawer scissors aiming to get even
prick her good. She bleeds a trail
as her fingernails shave bits of candle wax.
Its wick licks a match box
of hunkering brass tacks which turn on their heads
in self-defense. She coaxes
two hefty batteries into her poised flashlight.
Contact!

Light unfurls silky words from a hero
whose rough actions stop hearts. His betrothed goes after him
with his own blunt instrument,
her heart simply not in it. He sneezes, falls back
into love and gasps for forgiveness.

Picnic

My brother fishtailed along the gravel,
he and Dad debating the perfect tree
along the lake, until Dad yelled, *HERE*.
As they untied the trunk, my new friend
and I lined up like leaf ants to pass
fried chicken, potato salad, flaky biscuits,
and an icy watermelon which kept
Dad's cold beer upright in the cooler.
Each barking orders as we giggled
behind fanned-out hands, rolling our eyes.
My birthday cake above our heads,
we swiped a dollop of gooey chocolate
until one of us dropped it —icing first—
in the coarse stones crunching underfoot.
We froze as if hearing, *Simon Says*.
When my brother raised his hand
to lop off pebbled icing, blessing the cake
like Father McGregor, we giggled in relief.
Dad cursed, muttering, *wasted store-bought,*
adding to his list: *double night shift,*
damn kids—then paused to look
across the lake as if our mother would
float back. He refused to eat with us
as he downed beer, all those bottles
falling and rolling along the grass
and then he bowled our melon at the tree,
its trunk only slowing the inevitable
plop into the lake before splitting
into two halves which bobbed before
going around the bend. My brother took off
on foot through the trees. Dad veered home
as we pouted in the back seat
over our loss—icing, watermelon.

Maternal Instinct

I was sweeping when I first caught
sight of a Yellow Jacket lifting
from delicate petals in our newly-hung wallpaper
to hover near my eyebrow. It buzzed up into my hairline.
Reflexively I swatted the wasp with my hand
before soundly thrashing it
flat against the top window so hard
I shattered
glass. With cotton swabs
I carefully combed through broom straw
to find evidence, papery wings,
pale bent legs, that butter-soft body,
the stinger I so feared.
Frightened, in my fifth month of Lamaze,
I had exhaled rhythmically as I shoved
shards onto the blooming gardenias
whose fragrance soon drifted in
just above a rattling air conditioner
which shimmied and exhaled
into the flowering back yard.
With halting breath I peeked out
then lowered the thin window shade so that
its hem rested just above the shaking window unit.
The flimsy pale shade swelled then flattened
then rounded out, slowing
my uneven breaths.

Fire!

At 4 a. m. I walk through
water thigh-deep, living room-wide.
I side-step axes, massive hands
and hip boots that move against
a tide that laps against our staircase
then slaps my legs. More than once I buckle,
which makes my daughter laugh in my ear
all the way out to the sidewalk where
her daddy-long-leg nudges the back of
my knee. More soft laughter. *Mommy,
again.* As if I were helping her swing higher
higher. I turn her away from men
riding hoses aimed at nearby roofs
while the stunned homeless gawk
at all we had going up in smoke.
Just above, a figure flaps like paper
from the last rung of an imposing ladder
backlit by flames. My child points at
spots clustered along the power line, a family
of plump caws that she counts out.
She giggles, begins again.

Heat Wave

Beads cling
then slip from my lip like drops

on the rim of the inert hose
as firemen brace for

the mule-kick that never comes.
Comical if my house weren't

just beyond reach. I scraped hard for
planed boards, fresh paint,

solid roof. Yet chance chased gasoline
with a cartwheeling match.

Fifth Anniversary

He proved both right and wrong
most of the time, which led to arguments
I internalized. What was I
but prop, the fairer self?
I played advocate to this culprit
who drew and repelled.
If he were devil, I served as alter-ego
tripping over the hem of his scarlet robe
as he burnt brisket
the dog coughed up
after we fell upon each other,
sharp knife vying with its vital
jabbing fork. For our cause célèbre,
we camped out in the rocky backyard,
spooning through a tunnel
of expletives. Truth
stretched our lean-to, balance shifting
with his abrading exhale.
Whenever I revered him,
he would slip a notch. If he fell
or was pushed by those who loved him most,
I would extend my hand
and he would pull me through
delusion. How we did roll, tussle,
embrace. Comrades in arms.

Appropriate

I love the dodge, ruse, subterfuge,
the something of yours which will be mine.
Nothing personal, always business,
someone else's, which quickens my pulse
like some employer rushing to deal
with a thief, this little thief,
my throbbing head jam-packed
with the best pilfered goodies I don't need.
Well, the mind is overpowering.
Just tell yourself you have already
been in, your ticket misplaced.
Saunter past the bored docent,
match the smile, slow a bit,
that's disarming. They advance only if
you speed through or tense up.
Glide and woo, it's a shoe-in.
Claim the best seat in someone else's
house. Let them entertain you.

To break the silence

I wander the dim-lit neighborhood to watch
how others socialize. Up the block
dinner party guests gather,
drinks in hand.
Every so often someone breaks
then glides toward another tight cluster.
A female tilts her head, listening intently while the man
boasts over another's squared shoulder.
One woman studies the carpet.
Is it hers?
Does she have carpet
envy, too? Is this somebody's husband
hers? Emphatically he drills a point lost on her.
She starts when chatting women throw
back their heads, laugh.
The hostess—too smartly dressed
to be wait-staff—advances with a tray of
nibbles I can't quite taste. She makes eye contact,
adroitly urging a napkin
into a guest's palm. This does the trick. Tidbits float
from tray to hand outstretched.
Smooth. I mimic her poise
beneath a valanced window, my hip swishing
my imaginary Donna Reid skirt
draped in moonlight the color of whiskey,
neat. I pirouette, tray extended, offing,
Do try this. Then I pivot,
becoming other, smile, accept.

Come Saturday

I would drink in *Casamento's* night life,
a backsplash of blue on tile
floor, walls, ceiling.

                Dock workers, blue-faced.
The regulars rocked back on bar stools to slide down a raw oyster
or upend a Dixie. A sea of faces listed toward the barkeep
or one another, reckless tipping on weak-kneed stools
soon to collapse.

                A snowy black-and-white
tv loomed over loners who looked up warily. Nearby, couples
gestured wildly, as if the Mighty Mississippi were
almost in reach.

                Aloof women chain-smoked and
smoldered. The cat burglar twins wore black pants and
turtlenecks, their lacquered beehives cobalt.

On this night, both brood over something. Nothing
alike, really, the left-handed twin, fresh-baked
baguette. Her sister, dry crust salvaged
for bread pudding.

                Their beaus scan
the pool table as if the night's still young. The twins
gut them with one long glare.

Downcast,
        both men,
                blue.

Suburban Tremors

I lilt and drop through a hilly neighborhood
where others play overwrought need on wide-screen

bay windows. Anything resembling my past life
I pass by quickly. No need for reruns. I linger instead

for pitches that drift from a slack-jawed window,
a cello moaning low then lower, each vaulted groan

barely clearing the stiff lip of trembling glass
upstairs. Each note scuffs, pretending this does not hurt

one bit as it scrapes and grates the pavement
then tumbles into an unmade bed full of weeds.

A Child Again
>   after viewing the Dutch film *The Vanishing*

I lean forward to meet the flame at center frame
engulfed in darkness. My eyes adjust.

A red silken backdrop falls forward. The heroine's elbows fan out
against the casket that hems her in.

My feet press the floor. Her trembling makes the spark waver
then go out.

Will she catch a whiff of chloroform beneath her quivering upper lip?
Again she flicks

her lighter, its flame held close enough to scorch the fabric
of fear. Her low groan

makes me shudder. The camera cuts to the fresh-turned ground
she lies beneath.

From moving upright to buried alive. I can't breathe! My own elbows
measure left, right.

I'm twelve again, reading burial tales under thick covers
by flickering flashlight.

Her tremble risks setting silk on fire. Be still. Don't waste oxygen.
Wait.

Nothing sounds

like a tin can rolling down the street
except its mate,

wanting to be stopped. A breeze lifts
sandwich paper,

gives tin a tumble. That sound!
How can a small

cylinder echo so? Nightfall douses
sharp corners.

Tall dark overlords carry well-lit
gas cans and

whisper into unpeopled buildings,
fire! fire!

Fluorescent lighting on the fritz
pining to be

quarter-moon someday, some
cloudless night.

Dust swivels through corridors
growing bored

by infrequent winds. Alley stains
at sunrise.

Alternate Route

A pale figure in white
disappears into a blizzard of
indifference, a hamlet, nothing much
standing out against a powdery backdrop.
Terrain with no fence line links signposts
stripped of purpose. Bird droppings
on a crudely drawn letter *p*
leave the meaning of No Tres ass
to those who don't need signs.
At the county dump turnoff,
bleached sandwich wrappers brush
against a silo, its roof flapping a worn toupee.
One steadfast spindly tree,
a damp toothpick stuck to a nickel
in this coin purse left for trash.

Imagine

I'm peeking in on my family now
that I've gone. The household prospers.
Each one sways like wheat along goldenrod
walls. There's room enough to stretch up
and out.

      How routine it had all seemed
long ago, all gunmetal grey, a sleek quiet
vacuum.

      Something in their grace says
there is only this world, this day. One half-buried
photo, small glimmer of what or when I had been,
no sense or absence, really, nothing akin
to mourning or loss.

            As if whatever I touched
had been folded in like cinnamon in yellow
cake batter. Stir, erase.

Census Bureau

The trick is walking into my shadow
and not coming out. Or better yet,
gathering it around myself like a faded blanket
one folds carefully, outstretched arms
tucked in, the length longer than
I am tall. I have folded,
wanting no one to notice the direction I take
as I hunker behind landmark structures
the sun beats down upon. *Sweat it out,*
I tell myself. The moon will surface
to make its full case. Thus far it hasn't
cratered into earth, into me. A flashlight
could do me in, though in truth, the hand, arm,
face of its ghoulish inquisitor could make
my spirit vanish without a trace.

Doubt

I spot your animated face at our favored sunset table,
        slow my car to a crawl, then decide to circle the block.

Have I conjured you, there where I waited for you,
        track lighting glinting off our port? Just who is this

companion? Is this really you? So soon? Surely this man
        cocks his head like you had, lush locks flirting with

his high brow. And your new companion laughs as I
        once had. My second, third time past the plush setup,

I feel foolish. Why do I slow to this pacemaker pace
        that could draw attention? Will you spot my auto?

A fourth time around the block our willowy waiter
        bends over your strong shoulder, tops your bowl,

blocking my view. I think, *this is stalking*. You scan
        the ill-lit dining room, only half listening to her inane

monologue. Oh, but you could absorb atmosphere
        while making others feel special. Stalking, yes,

I confess. You reach out gently, slowly, for your glass,
        not her hand. She sighs. I hear it through double-ply

glass. That's when I gasp. A truck riding my bumper
        honk-honks, startling the waiter and then you, who

glance out at stalled-out stalking me. I peel away.
        Does she deflate in that comfy Bordeaux chair?

A blushing sunset can't make one plus one a twosome.

Quicksilver

When I find myself
reaching up to brush away

the curl teasing your eyelash—
mere reflex— you pull back.

We both note your body
refusing to be swayed

by me. Too close, this
intimate embarrassment.

This moment, the last
rapturous air we share.

I hold my breath. You
inhale evenly, intact.

Afterglow

Your eyes are diamonds, voice gravelly as rust,
      as you promise

to stay in touch, only this proves too much. (Silence)
      Years have passed

since we discussed why I fell out of love—
      too painful for

either of us. Memory makes fools of us. (More silence)
      We both knew

this could be a plus. For both of us. Yet here you are kicking up a fuss.
      We relive who

pushed who first. Something about diamonds and
      lust that turned

into dust. Choice thrust much on us. (Long silence) You say I made you
      ill but you were

always that way. Stardust abrades my abiding trust
      to the grave.

Foolish Endeavor

Try to outsmart
a skittery thing
whose very life depends
on your feeling nothing
of its delicate landing.
A butterfly-soft alight that stings
as it lifts up and away,
your tasty blood type
helicoptered
for fertility
by the time you reach down
to brush aside
that ticklish knowing,
that itch,
and it finds another
naked spot, another
limb you can't defend
quite quickly enough.
Why pretend, why
go through the motions.

Irresistible Full Moon

To test his pronouncement,
we threw a dim-lit party at the apex of what I term
Harvest Moon. Floor-to-ceiling

curtains framed a luminous
night sky. Twinkling candlelight glinted off glasses
of Chardonnay. Goblets of Merlot

in nearby shadows stood untouched.

Our friends stood mesmerized,
backs to the room where a lone guest had cratered.
Had he lost a loved one?

I started toward him when I felt
my love's pull, his kiss on my bright hand. *You're
aglow,* he'd said. And now,

bathed in illumination, I am breathless,

wobbly, as if he had just
tipped against my shoulder. Where he now rests
must be awash in light.

Rupture

Why make memories
when every incident in my head
plays
      not exactly

how I see things
but precise and unique in the way
my world is
      solely mine,

defined by what
makes me both sigh and laugh at
crass disaster
      befalling *Daphnia*,

a common water flea
that blunders past *Utricularia*,
a swaying lush
      water flower

that flaunts its rapture
to imprison naïve prey. *Daphnia*
probes another
      and digests

her dilemma. Eaten
by an acidic rootless flytrap,
a commoner,
      Bladderwort.

Like my daughter

long ago moving in my womb,
I slowly stretch one leg then the other, toes pressing
against bedsheets holding me in place.

Each ball in turn presses, persistent
as when she explored the confines of her tight quarters,

each tiny foot's imprint a tease
then retreat against my taut belly. With lax calves I swing
my feet onto cool surface, *terra firma*.

A mother herself now, her long
strong stride explores her world through hiking, walking,

half-marathons soon embedded
in memory. Her daughter now stretches toward finish lines,
lean limbs in motion even in sleep.

Flickering Prayer

Where have you gone, my other half?
Oh light, oh grace, oh shifting frame of reverence.
Still I've no one

as memory pales, misplaced. My body, my
spirit, please. Don't abandon me. Offhand glances
shift up, across

to others, some device. Games. I miss
having someone to tussle with. Having someone.
I miss that spark

you saw in me. I knew you'd grasp
a coaxing hand, wayward waif, not glancing back.
How I scrambled,

bereft. I'm here and there as I move on,
remain with you even though you passed through
then passed away.

Why go to heaven

if I can cross Napoleon
and head up Magazine Street for
a slice of T. Eva's sweet potato pie.
Or maybe I would see
in the cool of her converted snowball stand
a dark smooth misshapen praline.
Or paper-thin skins curling away from red beans
so plump I cradle one at a time
on my tongue. Juices in the Styrofoam bowl
moisten rice expertly steamed. Perfect
timing before she sells out,
before the Mardi Gras revelers shift focus
from catching doubloons
to sampling a hot bowl of gumbo
like no one else can cook,
each spoonful a trombone solo
toward heaven.
I recall my daughter bite gingerly
into a crawfish pie, crust so flaky
I want to chicken dance
all the way back to the parade route.
I meet myself strolling with my ex—
inappropriate timing, here in
twilight memory—as he presses
index finger to his thumb,
an OK sign spiraling pot plumes,
hands still greasy from repair work when
that season's celebrity, Elvis, lost his head
to power lines, his legendary sneer scraping concrete
like a full-blown overdose. We floated home
in our Caddy the color of soiled cotton,
the paper mache King gazing back
through the open trunk at the slack-jawed
fool riding our bumper so close
he might graze our beads.

Origin of Reason

Her look passes through me
to something I don't want
to see beyond. I turn
to confirm that I do not cause
her horrified yet haughty look. That thing
she greets, eight heads, foul breath

and one piercing eye, proves that
nightmares survive. Thrive. All this resides
in my seven-year-old mind
that in my sixth decade
begs the same soft question,
am I safe?

I am

my father stumbling stiff-legged
in darkness, minus the lit cigarette
announcing where he sat, thinking

or not, about sleep, or its lack, or life,
and that great loss we lived with, a mother,
wife, who finally slept after waiting.

For what, no one fathomed. I could not
idle at a formica table facing a large
white clock whose sweeping hands moved

too slowly and loud. Once for spite
I moved the little hand back twenty-three
minutes. It changed a lot, for she

reached out—perhaps in the dark—
and made right what I had wronged.
How is it I am not so generous?

As she inhabits my arthritic knees
creaking in an inviting lobby in a posh
hotel so far from anyone I know,

I sense she is with me, within me,
staring back at strangers who observe
this solitary older woman. What

would they know? With that first slap
stirring breath, we are—each of us—

on our own.

Fifty-Minute Therapy Session: Formative Years

She suggests I
take apart the wind-up clock called primary school
to see how this works.

Sharp faces face off.
Gears mesh.

I drop each piece on the table. Close my eyes.
Try to put it back together.

How sharp, recall's rough teeth, its flecks of
so-what.

Save me from these tumble-down worn stairs
tick–tock
as if there's fidelity in mechanics. How to
tighten the escape wheel?

Scramble for that lost fragment stepped over in the night.

Whose home is there no place like?

No, after you.

I drift through recess where the proper time is ahead,
behind, never universal.

Lug this scuffed exterior with its alarming cracked face.

Missing knob?
Don't you mean nugget

I pocket a bent hand
then cradle its exposed backside with a stained polish cloth
for what feels

a never-ending short while.

I heard

quiet, nothing but,
as snow blanketed the lawns,
the streets, even the rail ties

that glinted and winked like
gold teeth beneath off-white slush
as our lumbering beige car
eased over the tracks.
I would lie awake, hearing
nothing, not even a passing flatbed,
until the 10:45 would
shimmy as it blew through.

At 10:50 our neighbor
would cast a shadow down the stairs
as if in a silent film
then coast his old wreck downhill

until it coughed into being
at bottom, turning left beyond the rails,
and arriving on time,
it would seem,
for his 11 o'clock shift
at the *Red White and Brew*.
I heard if you fed quarters to the jukebox
it would play on into first light.

Some drank there, I suppose, to blast out
thought, simply be. Perhaps a pounding rhythm
served as prelude or

soundtrack for something you made
happen. Or happened to you.
If I had been drinking age
I would have trudged back home
through the mute snow
simply to process all I had heard.
Back then, I had thought
I'd seen everything.

Unexpected Guest

Surely not here, not now, Mother,
though I see you as clearly as fifty years ago,
your back to the room, to me,
as you sit transfixed,
turning pages in a book you don't follow,
not really. I still wince at the thick damp hair
I could not touch. Are you here, now,
because I conjure you, or had I stared
for so long that the image of your bony discomfort,
you as fact, will never leave me. I smell
that dank sweat of your loose-fitting shirt
and I cough. Old times. The tight little room
threaded in smoke. I inhale just what
I inherit. Indifference. The present
made from endless beads having no past,
no future. You sit, crooked, unmoving,
as if posing. No, more likely, in shock.
Breath inhaled for a snapshot,
a momentous occasion no one
misses. Yet we did. I do. Miss it,
relive it, this nothingness strung out,
weak fibers hefting what feels heavy
but rises like smoke. Faux-bright
beads, pure nonsense, strung together,
flung off. Landing behind the stove
with its door ajar, its oven overheating,
a burner sitting cockeyed,
the pot sporting its jaunty cap.
Enough. Floorboards tipped back,
long and lean as a bowling alley,
a landslide inheritance. Stop.
Lost her marbles, I had once joked with
a playmate. To fit in. Once even rolling
my favorite marble to the door.
All the time in this world
to change course. Please. Go. Take this
with you. Back you go.

Sunset Aperitif in the Garden

I did well today, not reflecting on
the quality of my frayed life. How little
it would take to tip compound pleasure into a heap
of fragments, splintering an expectant day
into twigs and sticks choking the blue
borrowed mower, the day ballooning as
late-afternoon air swells this wading pool of want.
I hear a soft splat overhead. Two. Three
drops, heavy as labored breathing. I take in
cooler air, the day swelling
as drops pummel my *Alocasia Calidora Palm,*
its elephant ear leaves dipping
like an appetizer tray at a garden party,
or bereavement, where thoughts turn
inward and laughter tries
the confused bereft. Tears form a tipsy conga line
after vows. Soil to soul, life akimbo.

Bacchanal

While others peel back
snug grapefruit skin from its bitter innards,
she rolls one large blushing ball
in her palm, her stained nails a giveaway
that she would love to dig in. Yet she
forbears sour juices spilling down her blouse
and waits in line, almost patient,
her posture a form of care,
her mind clocking distance against time,
how long the route to kitchen counter
where she can coddle this ripe wonder
in her best oversized bowl,
halve it then trace each section with
serrated knife. Sprinkle brown sugar. Scoop
a mouthful, more. Flatten pulpy half-ball. Lift
to upturned face. Swallow. Wipe chin
with back of hand.